# "Recharging My Soul"

# By: Ma'Sheka Amina Thomas

© 2018 Recharging My Soul Ma'Sheka
Amina Thomas

All rights reserved. This book may not be reproduced in whole or in part, or transmitted in any form, or by any means electronic, mechanical, photocopying, recording, or other, without written permission from the publisher, except by a reviewer who may quote brief passages in a review.

ISBN: 978-1-387-82698-8

First Printing: August 2018

Printed in the U.S.A

Thank you, God for the opportunity to step out on faith and for the people you have placed in my life.

I AM extremely grateful.

## **Foreword**

In a world where everything is draining you, from work to relationships, to small details in between, there has to be a day for you. A day where you can do absolutely nothing, but simply be and be thankful for where you are. Some people use Sundays for self-care, some choose another day. Many never have the opportunity to stop and take any "me time".

Don't let this be you. This was me for a long time. Until I stopped and realized that I had to recharge. I learned to do so through writing poems, affirmations, and messages.

Find a day to recharge your soul.

To recharge is to do things that make you happy. When you are feeling empty, find a way to reconnect. It is not selfish to allow yourself to give yourself, as much as pour out into others.

You Matter.

You take this time to make you feel whole.

To give you that spark.

Everyone needs a little recharge. Read for yourself, take what you need, then pass along to someone else.

# INSPIRATION

## **Inspiration**

My ability to journal has led me to my writings, blogging, and creating this book. I knew most of the things I did not like but was still trying to figure out what exactly did I like. Through the power of writing, letting go of anything that was not aligned with who I am, and reflecting on my experiences, I was encouraged to create. Picking up a pen and paper was the first part of the journey.

Sometimes inspiration does not come easy. We all could use some inspiration as I too become inspired by others.

I hope you will be able to find inspiration for whatever you may be seeking.

## To the talented and the creatives

I like what I like

Not asking you for your opinion

Because I like what I like

I am open to your view when needed

But I like what I like

I will not allow you to mess up my perception of what I deem to be beautiful

Thank you for your advice

But I see greatness when I see it

If you do not appreciate my art that I created for today

I can assure you will tomorrow.

To the talented and the creatives;

keep creating.

**Affirmation:**
- I like what I like.
- I AM a unique individual.

**Your Own Affirmation:**
- _____

# Out the box

You are not that 9 to 5 job
You are limitless
Fearless
You can create
Don't worry about the naysayers

Boss. Entrepreneur. Free. Bold.
Mental clarity and ideas flowing
Continue to walk in your purpose.

**Affirmation:**
- I AM creative.
- I AM limitless.
- I AM fearless.

**Your own Affirmation:**
- _____

# **Be...**

Inspired.

Self-motivated.

Bold.

Confident.

Selfless.

Selfish.

Kind.

Nice.

Encouraged.

Encourager.

A friend.

You.

**Affirmation:**
- I AM still and at peace.

**Your own Affirmation:**
- _____

# ...is key.

Consistency

Persistence

Happiness

Moving forward

Understanding

Loving yourself

Minding your business

Being kind

Enjoying life

Being yourself

Trying

Being thankful

Patience

Love

Is key to a joyous fulfilling life.

**Affirmation:**
- I AM balanced and centered.
- I AM living my best life.

**Your own Affirmation:**
- _____

# Time

The time is now

Not tomorrow

Today

Right now

The timing is always right

What is meant to happen will happen

24 hours

Use it wisely

Spend it with your family

Yourself,

Your friends

Value it

You can never get it back

Time

Heals.

**Affirmation:**

- I use my time wisely.

**Your own Affirmation:**

- _____

# Hustle

For anything you want you have to Hustle.
Hard work will you get you far

Do you know why you are here?
Why you do what you do?
Are you satisfied?

If not,
Make a change.

Hustle until you know you fulfilled your God given purpose.
Hustle until you know you're financially stable.
Hustle until you know your family is good.
Hustle until you know you reached generational wealth.
Don't give up! You got this!

**Affirmation:**
- I AM disciplined in all areas of my life.
- I AM a hard worker.

**Your own Affirmation:**

_____

# **What makes you feel good?**

Me?

You?

Food?

Traveling?

Solitude?

Being surrounded by your partner?

Children?

Family?

Friends?

Making someone day?

Someone else making your day?

Waking up in the morning?

Coffee?

Working out?

Being alive?

Hiking?

Shopping?

Creating music? Creative projects?

Completing your to-do-lists for today?

Losing weight?

Have you thought about this?

What makes you feel good?

**Affirmation:**
- I do things to make me happy.

**Your own Affirmation:**
- _____

## **I AM me**

I AM an example,

Striving to fulfill my purpose.

I AM the change I want to see, sending love to other people.

I AM using my skills to uplift those around me

I AM in control

I can manifest great things into my life

I AM Powerful

I AM the change I want to see

No fear allowed here

I AM Powerful being

The light shining so bright on me.

I AM me and there is no one like me.


**Affirmation:**
- I love who I AM.

**Your own affirmation:**

_____

# You are...

You are smart

You are intelligent

You are beautiful

You are bold

You are a leader

You are kind

You are loving

You are a blessing

You are imaginative

You are happiness

You are joy

You are peace

You are art

You were a masterpiece

Since Birth

**Affirmation:**
- I AM happy and filled with joy.

**Your own Affirmation:**
- _____

YOU are more than enough.

Stop comparing yourself to others.

Stop being so critical of yourself.

YOUR time is YOUR time.

When you are going through trying times, don't give up on your faith, just know a storm of blessings is about to rain down.

**Affirmation:**
- You are enough.

**Your own affirmation:**
- _____

## You're more than...

...a hello and goodbye.
...a gift.
..." you're beautiful" once a blue moon.
...what he gives.
...what she gives.
...a text when someone needs you.
... once in a while phone call.

## Because....
you deserve the greatest love.
you deserve peace and serenity.
you are the most the beautiful creature crafted by God.

You are worth it. You are enough.

**Affirmation:**
- I AM enough.

**Your own Affirmation:**

# Thank you!

2 words.

They mean a lot.

Thank you.

Thank you for all that you have done for me.

Your words stick with me.

Your actions please me.

You motivate me to do better.

Allow me to see what God has given me.

Thank you.

**Affirmation:**
- I AM thankful.

**Your own Affirmation:**
- _____

# **Back to Writing**

I took a break accidentally
Trying to heal myself mentally
See I'm trying to dig into my history of feelings
To understand why I react, respond, and do the things that I do
My truth,
Started with my grandmother,
Then my mother
Now me.
Each day I get it
The hurt
The pain
The disbelief
The expectation
I could go on
But I find myself writing
I discover my deepest fears and emotions
I cried
Sadness
Then joy
Amazing feeling to bring up my deepest emotions
But to feel relief that everything is okay
Forgive me for why I stop
And appreciate me for giving you more of me.

**Affirmation:**
- I take time out with me.
- I AM patient with myself and others.

**Your own Affirmation:**
- _____

# Notes to Self

## **Notes to self**

This is the advice that I give to others that I most often need myself. With these messages, I was able to talk myself through situations to help me grow, learn, and even unlearn. These are the messages I needed to hear to navigate through growing pains, relationships, and more.

# Exercising your mind.

When things get tough, know that everything will be okay. Feed your mind with positivity, so that you can manifest the great things you desire into your life. Be bold, and courageous with your decisions. Know that you are never alone for God is always with you. Life is a journey. Everything is working for your good. Ask God for His will and order your steps and everything will be alright.

**Affirmation:**

- All is great.

**Your own Affirmation:**

- _____

# **Work hard**

It does not matter what or who you are working for, get up every day to do something. Do not sit around. You have to move. Work out. Start your business. Invest. Go to school.

Try to surround yourself with winners and people who have things going for their selves. This can inspire you and allow your creative mind to flow.

Work hard so that it will pay off tomorrow.

**Affirmation:**

- I AM a hard worker.

**Your own Affirmation:**

- _____

# The only person you can control is *you*.

You cannot help what people say, but you can help how you respond. People will try to test you. Ignore the negativity. It's crazy the things people will do to push you out of character.

Think before you speak, for words are powerful and can not be taken back.

If you do get out of character: pray and let it go. You are changing, every second and every minute. You are growing. There will be mistakes, keep learning yourself.

**Affirmation:**

- I AM calm and centered.

**Your own Affirmation:**

- _____

# Things to try in life:

- Travel to another state
- Cook a new dish
- Traveling out the country
- Amusement park
- Moving to another state
- New food
- New restaurant
- Talking to a stranger
- Changing jobs
- Taking chances
- Thrifting
- Comedy show
- Go to a concert
- Write a short story
- Meditating
- Hot yoga
- Dance class

Try things you "wouldn't do". It might bring out characteristics that you never knew you have. We need more people who are willing to try things. Trying something new can make a huge difference in your life and those surrounding you.

**Affirmation:**

- I AM open to trying new things in life.

**Your own Affirmation:**

- _____

## **Control**

As much as we would love to control things, we cannot. Once we try, it seems like everything goes wrong. Make plans but allow The Creator to guide you to your heart greatest desires. He already knows how things are going to go. High expectations lead to big disappointments. More control that you try to have, the less patience you harness. If you want something to happen, more than likely you want it to happen on your terms…perfect time and place. Whatever you desire, the moment will be more than the moment after you let go and let God.

Remember: You can always control what you do or say, but you cannot control others.

**Affirmation:**

- I AM able to control my thoughts and emotions.

**Your own Affirmation:**

- _____

# Going with the flow

There's nothing wrong with having a plan, but prepare your mind for when things go left. Remember what happens is meant to happen. There was a reason why things didn't go as planned. Trust the process. Sometimes the plan you didn't create has the best outcome.

Detach yourself from all the plans you are connected to.

Going with the flow makes life less complicated.

**Affirmation:**
- I AM flowing.

**Your own Affirmation:**
- _____

# **Life:**

Be compassionate and understanding of people.

Their actions, their past, and their present.

Know that not everyone intends are to hurt you.

When you have grasped the idea

of life you'll see there is beauty in the struggle.

So much that it has to offer

You may have ups and downs,

Find appreciation in life

It's beautiful.

Everywhere you go just allow things to flow.

Know who you are and do not take yourself too seriously.

Everything will be okay.

We are meant to make mistakes, learn, and grow from them.

Life is meant to be a beautiful chaos.

Be aware, but also compassionate.

Change your perspective and allow positivity to attract you.

**Affirmation:**

- I AM understanding of self, love, and others.

**Your own Affirmation:**

- _____

When you can't sympathize with a person
just be quiet.
Try to find understanding and lose judgement.

**Affirmation:**

- The words I speak have value.

**Your own Affirmation:**

- _____

# Insecurities

We all have insecurities deep inside of us. They creep up on us every now and then. Sometimes, people you encounter or circumstances that bring them to the surface. Reflect where they stem from. Analyze that feeling. If it doesn't feel good, figure out why.

**Affirmation:**

- I AM secure with who I AM.

**Your own Affirmation:**

- _____

# **Living your truth**

If you're living in your truth:

    no one can break you
    you will feel free
    you will let it go
    you'll be comfortable to talk about it, perhaps build a platform
    acceptance of self but also acceptance
    live your best life

**Affirmation:**

- I AM living in my truth.

**Your own Affirmation:**

- _____

# Patience + Persistence

Anything you want in life, you must be persistent and patient. It is the key to success. As much as you talk about it, you should pray about it. When you pray about it, continue to work for it, and wait patiently. Trust God's timing. Take your time. It takes hard work, persistence, motivation, and a lot of prayers. You can not pray about it and have no action behind it.

**Be persistent, but also patient.**

Proverbs 14:23:

"All hard work brings a profit, but mere talk leads only to poverty".

Psalm 37:

Be still before the Lord and wait patiently for him; do not fret when people succeed in their ways, when they carry out their schemes.


Affirmation:
- I AM patient with self, love, and others.

Your own Affirmation:
- _____

# Power of Prayer
## Pray for:

Perseverance

Clarity

Patience

Direction

Peace

Yourself

Family

Love and wealth

For God continue to shine his light through you and use you to fulfill your purpose

And of course, pray for those that don't wish you well

**Affirmation:**
- The Creator is within me.
- I AM grateful.

**Your own Affirmation:**
- _____

# Everything will be just fine

Know that everything is going to work out in your favor. It's going to be alright. You'll pass your class and do other things that you need to do. Your business will strive. Just make sure you're always keeping God first through everything. He will help and guide you to the right people. You must have faith. Trust that things will work out. Do not stress. There's no need to complain. Remember someone always has it worst and is working harder than you without any complaints. You really don't have it bad. Stay focused! Love everyone. Keep God first and you'll be okay. Trust me. You are smart and dedicated. You are a hustler. You are going to do well in school, your career, your craft, and whatever you put your mind to. Just put the work in and don't let people deter you away from the goal.

**Affirmation:**
- Everything is okay.

**Your own Affirmation:**
- _____

# Keep Going

Although, it may seem like you have a lot going on just know anything is POSSIBLE. Keep your head up and stay away from distractions. You'll find yourself doing so much more and having so much more time. Give thanks to The Creator for everything you have been blessed with. Be thankful and grateful for your situation, it could be so much worse. Stay positive during your journey. It is going to have trying times, but remember the journey will be rewarding. Life is not hard, we just make it complicated. Roll with the punches and everything will be alright in the end. Keep your purpose in mind, head up, and pray knowing you've got this.
Positivity is key, keep going.

**Affirmation:**
- I AM present in all my endeavors.

**Your Own Affirmation:**
- _____

Be great.

In college, I started saying "Be Great". It came from me knowing I had the potential to be something greater. I believe people have so much potential but fail achieve it due to laziness. I always saw greatness in myself, so it allowed me to see greatness in others. There is so much to be done in this world. Why not strive to be great or yet your best self?

When I tell people to "be great", they tell me "I'm trying". Don't try, just do it. Be the greatest you. Don't half do anything, you'll get half results. Don't strive to be great like me, strive to be great like you. As God shines his light through me, I want to inspire others.

Understand that we ALL are capable of doing great things, we just have to get out there, do it, and surround ourselves with great people.

**Affirmation:**
- I AM Great.
- I have the abilities to be who I desire to be.

**Your own Affirmation:**
- _____

# Key Reminders

1. Your reaction is your responsibility.
2. Leave the past in the past.
3. Be great.
4. You have control over self.
5. Accept what is and move forward.
6. Just be yourself. If people like you, they do and if they don't God loves you anyway.
7. Be who you are.
8. Choose God to fight all your battles. For HE is stronger than you.
9. Never take it personal.
10. Always choose positivity.
11. Be happy.
12. Just because someone asks you a question doesn't mean they are entitled to an answer.
13. You always have a choice.
14. You're beautiful.
15. You are worthy.

# POSITIVE VIBES

## **Positive Vibes**

Having positivity in your life allows you to smile, be free, and allows room for things in your life to flow. It took time for me to be in a space of peace and being thankful for what I have. It's so easy to get caught up in things that do not matter.

As I was writing, it gave me the ability to reflect, reminisce, and let go of a lot of baggage that I was holding on to.

# You know what I love…

Peace of mind

the joy God brings me

the smell of fresh coffee in the morning

being able to wake up breathing

surrounding myself by nature's beauty

the taste of a sweet cake and tacos on a Tuesday

the joy I receive from life

the love that I continue to give myself

the feeling of love

being in the presence of you

**Affirmation:**
- I love life.

**Your own Affirmation:**
- _____

## **My Intentions are to:**

be best-selling author

love more

be more ambitious

be healthy, fit, and glowing

make an impact

be the light of the world

be a better person

inspire and uplift you.

## **Affirmation:**

- I have great intentions that are followed by my actions.

## **Your own Affirmation:**

- _____

# In Good Spirits

Happy
Filled with joy
I love waking up
And seeing the sun's ray
Another chance
To see and experience
Life is beautiful
I have a relationship with God
I love myself
And constantly discovering more of me
In this moment I have all that I need
Happy
I have the ability to uplift others
And understand my life's purpose
Happy
Is what I choose to be
It feels good to experience this feeling
And express through my writing
I pray we all arrive in this state of being.

**Affirmation:**
- I AM happy and filled with joy.

**Your own Affirmation:**
- _____

# **In this present moment...**

Appreciating every minute

Loving everyone around

Being thankful

For this one life

The life that we were blessed with

To have choices and endless opportunities

My days filled with many highs and very little lows

Being where I need to be

Feeling like royalty

Because I've been blessed

With this moment

And so have you.

**Affirmation:**

- I appreciate love.

**Your own Affirmation:**

- _____

# "Hey baby, you need a hug?"

Life is taking a toll on me
It seems like you always know
I guess to you, it always shows
My emotions on my sleeve
Just need that extra push
Being embraced in your arms
So, yes I need that hug
Filled with your unconditional love

**Affirmation:**
- I deserve love and affection.

**Your own affection:**
- _____

# Balanced

I AM balanced

I AM not silent

Ying and Yang

Something I try to perfect everyday

To become very centered in my thoughts

Want to be remembered

For being great

Don't want to be stagnate

Because that would be tragic

But I pray

That there will be more highs than lows

I laugh

I cry

I feel

A new balance

**Affirmation:**
- I AM walking into my increase.

**Your own Affirmation:**
- _____

# Untitled

Words have power
You have power
All you have to do is say it
It's already inside of you
Find it
Reach it
Hold on to it
Do not let ANYONE try to take it away
You worked too damn hard

**Affirmation:**
- My words have power.
- I AM powerful.

**Your own Affirmation:**
- _____

# **Chocolate**

Sweet as pie.
Sexy as Kofi Siriboe.
Sensational as my first thought to describe you.
Strong as you hold me so tightly.
Sincere as you listen to my thoughts and fulfill my every need.
Smart as all the knowledge within the books I read.
and most importantly made especially for me.

**Affirmation:**

- I attract relationships to me that are for the highest good of all.
- I give and receive love freely and fully in all my relationships.

**Your own Affirmation:**

- _____

# Dreams

I dream about you often
Mostly your love
Sometimes it's you caressing my body
Other times you're speaking to my mind
Leading me to the right direction
Which is you
I am awakened with all smiles
Even you appearing in my dreams,
Makes me have a great day.

**Affirmation:**
- My imagination allows me to create.

**Your own Affirmation:**
- _____

# **Naturally you**

Naturally you

Authentic

Gracious

Hair naturally coily

Smelling so good

Feeling so soft

Cocoa butter skin

Sun kissed

Melanin

Face radiant and clear

Laughing as loud as I could because

I AM in love with me.

**Affirmation:**
- I AM me.

**Your own Affirmation:**
- _____

# My Own Hypeman

You are so beautiful

Your smile

Your love that you give

You make life worthwhile

Your personality

Only one of one

So easy to be you

Real cool

Many skills and great qualities

Becoming your best self

Bold and courageous

With a hint of crazy

Never lazy

Always fine and smelling like a daisy

Girl, I Love you

Remember to love yourself

                You can always depend on me,

                    Your Hypeman

**Affirmation:**
- I AM me.
- I AM the best version of me.
- There's only one of me.

**Your own Affirmation:**
- _____

I AM not what you think I AM.

I AM still growing.

# Transitions

## **Transitions**

Every day we are striving to be a better version of ourselves and creating a new lifestyle that fits who we are at that time. We are constantly trying to create good habits that will help us during our journey. Creating new habits is not always easy. There are times when we are transitioning into this new and improved person, hard work will be involved. In the meantime, be aware, let go, forgive, and move onward and forward with your life.

The transitions in our lives are happening as you read. Some things we have no control over, however, we have control of our actions, thoughts, and the words we speak.

Get to know you even if it's not all good. What good is it for someone to know you, if you don't know yourself?

# Inquisitive.

How do you express yourself?

Are you afraid of confrontation?

Do you always have to be happy?

Can there be a moment of sadness?

Is it ever that serious?

Have you ever lost your faith?

Do you think you deserve more than you settle for?

Why do we seek validation from others?

What am I afraid of?

What troubles your soul?

What does your heart desire?

You cannot stop destiny or things from happening, so why do you continue to stress over things you have no control over?

**Affirmation:**
- All the questions I seek, the answers already exist within me.

**Your own Affirmation:**
- _____

# **Conflicted**

Help me God, help me

For this is a feeling that no one should bear

I keep telling myself to be fearless

For I am strong

But what happens when others want you to dim your light

Because it's too bright

I feel that

I am walking on egg shells

Around you

You give me this feeling that I don't want to go back to

Conflicted

I wont be near you

I'll love you from a distance

Because I refused to be in this position

**Affirmation:**
- I AM able to feel how I feel without feeling guilty or shameful.

**Your own Affirmation:**
- _____

# See when I…

When I was dreaming
Your love felt so pure
I cared.
You cared.
There was no heartache
It was like nothing had ever happened.
So forgiveness had to be there
Because it felt so right

When I woke up
I knew it wasn't love
I cared about you leaving
You cared about fucking me
Such a heartache
Everything had happened
but I decided to forgive you
Because it was right
For me


**Affirmation:**
- I have the ability to forgive.

**Your own Affirmation:**
- _____

# Forgiveness

The hardest thing to do

But I give it to you anyway

For me

It's a spiritual healing

A good feeling

A way to move forward

You have to forgive

Even when you don't want to

It's the best way to live.

**Affirmation:**

- It is possible to forgive myself and others.

**Your own Affirmation:**

- _____

# **Late night thoughts**

You gave up.

I didn't.

Can we really have a conversation on forgiveness?

You said that you "love" me.

Love

A word that gets thrown around too easily.

However…

I thank you.

For you have taught me everything I don't want…

You.

**Affirmation:**

- I AM able to reflect and release any negative emotions.

**Your own Affirmation:**

- _____

## **No more controlling**

You left
I asked you to stay
But I won't chase you

I AM letting go

God is in control
He got me
He got you

If it's meant to be
We will be one

No more controlling
What you do
Or what happens to us
There's no fuss

I've given you space
But I'll be in a different place
Growing and evolving
Still unconditionally loving
You

**Affirmation:**
- I let go and let God.
- I AM letting go the need to control.

**Your own Affirmation:**
- _____

# **Stop being judgmental**

Stop being so damn judgmental
I give you a piece of me
You throw it back in my face
Let's trade places
You wouldn't like if I did that to you
I am not that type of person
Those who judge are hurt
Since something is wrong with them
They want to find things wrong with me
I won't allow it into my space
Your problems are yours to face

**Affirmation:**
- I demand respect.

**Your own Affirmation:**
- _____

## Are you afraid?

of getting your heart broken?

of forgiving the same person who fucked you over several times?

of being open minded?

of leaving the job that you hate?

of moving to another state where there are endless opportunities?

of letting go?

of growing?

    What is meant to happen will.

    God is always protecting you.

So why are you still afraid?

**Affirmation:**
- I AM fearless.

**Your own Affirmation:**
- _____

# Patiently waiting

Working on myself

Becoming whole

Figuring out who I am

On many levels

Trusting me

Loving me

Respecting me

Honoring me

Daydreaming about the thoughts of you

I feel you are near

Appreciating the space I do have

Learning more about love

Giving love to me

Receiving love from you

Patiently waiting

**Affirmation:**

- I AM patient.

**Your own Affirmation:**

- _____

Don't feel like it

Don't feel like putting on makeup
Getting drunk
To come home
Alone
Take off the makeup
And wake up
With a hangover
To clean up
And say I'm not doing this again

I just don't want to go out
Not tonight
I just want to chill
Eat a nice cooked meal
Relax
Do nothing
I feel like I'm always doing something
Lay in bed

**Affirmation:**
- I only do things I desire to do.
- I feel good about the decisions I make.

**Your own Affirmation:**
- _____

# **Move**

You better move.

Stay still and watch:

Your life will turn into chaos.

Move forward and watch:

Your life will blossom into something so beautiful.

**Affirmation:**

- I accept change into my life

**Your own affirmation:**

- _____

# Questions

What troubles your soul?

Are you speaking life into your dreams?

What does your heart desire?

Do you accept your flaws and all?

Do you know what you want out of life?

Why do you do what you do?

How are you going to dominate?

Do you know you are great?

Did you make time for yourself today?

**Affirmation:**
- I accept me for me.

**Your own Affirmation:**
- _____

## Do YOU believe?

Do you believe in God?

Do you believe he can make the impossible possible?

Many times people say they believe and then doubt.

I have done it before and now when I look back I'm sure He was insulted. That's why I love God. He is forgiving and loving. God is love.

Believing in God equates to having faith that all things are working for your good even when you think it's not.

Constantly being reminded that there's always a blessing in disguise.

When you believe in God he shines his light through you.

My happiness is being filled with joy because joy is everlasting.

When people see your joy they want it too and wonder what's the secret. Well the secret is simply putting your life in God hands. He is in control. Once you put full control in God hands then you'll become content because you know it'll work out for your good. What's meant to happen will.

Have faith. Trust in God and believe.

**Affirmation:**
- I believe.

**Your own Affirmation:**
- _____

# The power of NO

The power of NO
You're allowed to say it
You're untitled to it
It's your will
It's your power
Do not let anyone make you feel bad for saying NO
Do not let anyone manipulate your NO
The power of NO
Use it
Empower it
Without apologies

**Affirmation:**
- I make decisions that are best for me.

**Your own Affirmation:**
- _____

# ...NOW

I feel your pain
In my heart
Everything will be okay
And I know they keep telling you that
But it is a fact
Growing pains
Things won't be the same
You will change
For the better
Stronger
Ready to take on the world
The best thing you are looking for
Now
Is strength and guidance
Patience
Solitude and creating your balance
Will help you heal
The wounds
So that your flowers can bloom

**Affirmation:**
- I understand the season I AM in.

**Your own Affirmation:**
- _____

I told you to wait for me.

*Your loss.*

Going up.
      Glowing up.
           Growing up.

**Affirmation:**
- I AM growing, learning, evolving.

**Your own Affirmation:**
- _____

# Growth

Growth
I am growing each and every day
Not looking back
Proud of me
Thankful for God blessing me with this gift
To be devoted to writing, speaking, and encouraging
My experience has allowed me to grow in ways I could not imagine
Thinking twice before I speak
Saying all that I need to say
Smiling knowing it is alright
And always letting my light shine
Growth

**Affirmation:**

I AM growing.

**Your own Affirmation:**

_____

**What if I told you that if you left your current situation, you could be able to experience many opportunities and joy in this new journey?**

**Would you take a chance?**

**Thank you, God for my life's experiences. Each one helped me create this masterpiece.
They have made me what "I AM".**

**To whomever is reading:**

**Remember you always get what your heart truly desires.**

**Be patient.**

**Peace, love, and light to you.**

# **Affirmations**

At the end of each piece, I shared my affirmations. In addition, I provided you with space to create your own. The power of affirmations has allowed me to grow and believe in my ability to speak things into my life. Start by saying affirmations once a day, then twice a day. Use the spaces to create what you need. My prayer is that these affirmations will help manifest your desires.

Enjoy!

Don't forget to recharge. Don't be too consumed with other things to check in and check up on yourself.

**Affirmations:**

I love who I AM.
I AM that I AM.
I AM able to control my thoughts and emotions.
I AM understanding of self, love, and others.
I love my personality.
I AM fearless.
I accept change into my life
I AM surrounded by loyal people.
I AM able to reflect and release any negative emotions.
I AM a walking into my greatest potential.
I AM secure with who I AM.
All the questions I seek, the answers already exist within me.
I AM me.
I create positive habits.
I love life.

I just love the energy I bring.
I AM still and at peace.

I AM open to trying new things in life.
I AM secure with who I AM and all that I AM.
I do things to make me happy.
I AM calm and center.
I AM a hard worker.
I love me.
I AM open to love.
I AM balanced and center.
I AM living my best life.
The beautiful things I see within myself, I see within others.
I eat foods that taste good and nurtures my body.
I AM able to feel how I feel without feeling guilty or shameful.
I deserve love and affection.
I AM me.
I AM the best version of me.
There's only one of me.
I AM thankful.

It is easy to forgive myself and others.
I AM a spiritual being.
I feel good about the decisions I make.
I only do things I desire to do.
I AM patient.
I AM a writer with a message.
I AM a great writer.
I demand respect.
I appreciate love.
I AM living in my truth.
I let go and let God.
I AM letting go the need to control.
I understand the season I AM in.
I like what I like.

I AM a unique individual.

I have great intentions that are followed by my actions.
I AM walking into my increase.

I AM happy and filled with joy.
I AM where I need to be.
I AM growing.
All is great.
I AM all that I AM.
I AM enough.
I AM at peace with what is.
I let go and let God.
I AM creative.
I AM limitless.
I AM fearless.
I AM growing, learning, and evolving.
I have a great support system.
I have the ability to forgive.
I AM enjoying this present moment.
I AM a risk taker.
My imagination allows me to create.
I enjoy the time I spend with myself.
I love the space I AM in.

I AM flowing.
I enjoy the feeling music gives me.
I AM patient with self, love, and others.
The creator is within me.
I AM thankful and grateful.
I AM great.
I have the abilities to be who I desire to be.
I use my time wisely.
I AM present in all my endeavors.
I accept me for me.
Everything is okay.
I AM disciplined in all areas of my life.
I AM a hard worker.
The words I speak have value.
I make decisions that are best for me.

Personal Affirmations
1.
2.
3.
4.
5.

Financial Affirmations
1.
2.
3.
4.
5.

Relationship Affirmations
1.
2.
3.
4.
5.

Social Affirmations
1.
2.
3.
4.
5.

Career Affirmations
1.
2.
3.
4.
5.

Spiritual Affirmations
1.
2.
3.
4.
5.

_____ Affirmations

1.
2.
3.
4.
5.

_____ Affirmations

1.
2.
3.
4.
5.